THE

Communion-Office,

OR ORDER

FOR THE ADMINISTRATION

OF THE

HOLY EUCHARIST

OR

SUPPER OF THE LORD.

WITH

PRIVATE DEVOTIONS.

Recommended to the Epifcopal Congregations in *Connecticut*,

By the Right Reverend
BISHOP SEABURY.

NEW-LONDON:
Printed by T. GREEN, M,DCC,LXXXVI.

Communion-Office.

¶ *The Exhortation.*

DEARLY beloved in the Lord, ye that
mind to come to the holy Communion
of the body and blood of our Saviour Chriſt,
muſt conſider how St. Paul exhorteth all per-
ſons diligently to try and examine themſelves,
before they preſume to eat of that bread, and
drink of that cup. For as the benefit is
great, if with a true penitent heart and lively
faith we receive that holy ſacrament, (for
then we ſpiritually eat the fleſh of Chriſt, and
drink his blood; then we dwell in Chriſt, and
Chriſt in us; we are one with Chriſt, and
Chriſt with us;) ſo is the danger great, if we
receive the ſame unworthily, not conſidering
the Lord's body; for then we are guilty of
the body and blood of Chriſt our Saviour; we
kindle God's wrath againſt us, and bring his
judgments upon us. Judge therefore yourſelves, brethren, that ye be not judged of the
Lord; repent you truly for your ſins paſt;

have

have a lively and ftedfaft faith in Chrift our Saviour; amend your lives, and be in perfect charity with all men: fo fhall ye be meet partakers of thofe holy myfteries. And, above all things, ye muft give moft humble and hearty thanks to God the Father, the Son, and the Holy Ghoft, for the redemption of the world, by the death and paffion of our Saviour Chrift, both God and man, who did humble himfelf even to the death upon the crofs for us miferable finners, who lay in darknefs and the fhadow of death, that he might make us the children of God, and exalt us to everlafting life. And to the end that we fhould always remember the exceeding great love of our Mafter and only Saviour Jesus Chrift thus dying for us, and the innumerable benefits which by his precious bloodfhedding he hath obtained to us, he hath inftituted and ordained holy myfteries, as pledges of his love, and for a continual remembrance of his death, to our great and endlefs comfort. To him, therefore, with the Father, and the Holy Ghoft, let us give (as we are moft bounden) continual thanks, fubmitting ourfelves wholly to his holy will and pleasure, and ftudying to ferve him in true holiness and righteoufnefs all the days of our life. *Amen.*

¶ *Then*

¶ *Then the Prieſt, or Deacon, ſhall ſay,*

Let us preſent our offerings to the Lord with reverence and Godly fear.

¶ *Then the Priest ſhall begin the offertory, ſay-ing one or more of theſe ſentences following, as he thinketh moſt convenient in his diſ-cretion.*

IN proceſs of time it came to paſs, that Cain brought of the fruit of the ground an offer-ing unto the Lord. And Abel, he alſo brought of the firſtlings of his flock, and of the fat thereof. And the Lord had reſpeſt unto Abel, and to his offering: but unto Cain and to his offering he had not reſpeſt. *Gen.* iv. 3, 4.

Speak unto the children of Iſrael, that they bring me an offering: of every man that gi-veth it willingly with his heart, ye ſhall take my offering. *Exod.* xxv. 2.

Ye ſhall not appear before the Lord empty. Every man ſhall give as he is able, according to the bleſſing of the Lord your God which he hath given you. *Deut.* xvi. 16, 17.

Give unto the Lord the glory due unto his name: bring an offering, and come into his courts. *Pſal.* xcvi. 8.

Lay not up for yourſelves treaſures upon earth, where moth and ruſt doth corrupt, and where thieves break through and ſteal: but

lay

lay up for yourſelves treaſures in heaven, where neither moth nor ruſt doth corrupt, and where thieves do not break through nor ſteal. *Mat.* vi. 19, 20.

Not every one that ſaith unto me, Lord, Lord, ſhall enter into the kingdom of heaven: but he that doth the will of my Father which is in heaven. *Matth.* vii. 21.

Jeſus ſat over againſt the treaſury, and beheld how the people caſt money into it: and many that were rich caſt in much. And there came a certain poor widow, and ſhe threw in two mites, which make a farthing. And he called unto him his diſciples, and ſaith unto them, Verily I ſay unto you, that this poor widow hath caſt more in, than all they which have caſt into the treaſury. For all they did caſt in of their abundance: but ſhe of her want did caſt in all that ſhe had, even all her living. *Mark* xii. 41, 42, 43, 44.

Who goeth a warfare at any time of his own charges? who planteth a vineyard, and eateth not of the fruit thereof? or who feedeth a flock, and eateth not of the milk of the flock? 1 *Cor.* ix. 7.

If we have ſown unto you ſpiritual things, is it a great matter if we ſhould reap your carnal things? 1 *Cor.* ix. 11.

Do ye not know, that they which miniſter about holy things, live of the ſacrifice? and they which wait at the altar, are partakers

with

with the altar? Even fo hath the Lord ordained, that they who preach the gofpel, fhould
live of the gofpel. 1 *Cor.* ix. 13, 14.

He that foweth fparingly, fhall reap alfo
fparingly: and he who foweth bountifully,
fhall reap alfo bountifully. Every man according as he purpofeth in his heart, fo let
him give; not grudgingly, or of neceffity: for
God loveth a chearful giver. 2 *Cor.* ix. 6, 7.

Let him that is taught in the word, communicate unto him that teacheth, in all good
things. Be not deceived; God is not mock-
ed: for whatfoever a man foweth, that fhall
he alfo reap. *Gal.* vi. 6, 7.

Charge them that are rich in this world,
that they be not high-minded, nor truft in
uncertain riches, but in the living God, who
giveth us richly all things to enjoy: That
they do good, that they be rich in good works,
ready to diftribute, willing to communicate;
laying up in ftore for themfelves a good foundation againft the time to come, that they may
lay hold on eternal life. 1 *Tim.* vi. 17, 18, 19.

God is not unrighteous, to forget your
work and labour of love, which ye have fhew-
ed toward his name, in that ye have minifter-
ed to the faints, and do minifter. *Heb.* vi. 10.

To do good, and to communicate, forget
not; for with fuch facrifices God is well pleafed. *Heb.* xiii. 16.

¶ *While*

¶ *While the Prieſt diſtinctly pronounceth ſome or all of theſe sentences for the offertory, the Deacon, or (if no ſuch be preſent) ſome other fit perſon, ſhall receive the devotions of the people, in a baſon provided for that purpoſe. And when all have offered, he ſhall reverently bring, and deliver it to the Prieſt; who ſhall humbly preſent it before the Lord, and ſet it upon the holy table, ſaying,*

BLESSED be thou, O Lord God, for ever and ever. Thine, O Lord, is the greatneſs, and the glory, and the victory, and the majeſty; for all that is in the heaven and in the earth is thine: thine is the kingdom, O Lord, and thou art exalted as head above all: both riches and honour come of thee, and of thine own do we give unto thee. *Amen.*

¶ *And the Prieſt shall then offer up, and place the bread and wine prepared for the ſacrament upon the Lord's table, putting a little pure water into the cup: and ſhall ſay,*

The Lord be with you.

Anſwer. And with thy ſpirit.

Prieſt. Lift up your hearts.

Anſwer. We lift them up unto the Lord.

Prieſt. Let us give thanks unto our Lord God.

Anſwer. It is meet and right ſo to do.

Prieſt. It is very meet, right, and our

bounden

bounden duty, that we ſhould at all times,
and in all places, give thanks
unto thee O Lord, * [holy   * *Theſe words* (holy
Father,] Almighty, everlaſt-   Father) *muſt be omit-*
ing God.   *ted on Trinity-Sunday.*

¶ *Here ſhall follow the proper preface, according to the time, if there be any eſpecially appointed ; or elſe immediately ſhall follow,*

Therefore with angels and archangels, &c.

¶ *Proper Prefaces.*

¶ *Upon Chriſtmas-day, and ſeven days after.*

BEcauſe thou didſt give Jeſus Chriſt thine
only Son, to be born * [as
on this day] for us, who, by the   * *During the*
operation of the Holy Ghoſt,   *ſeven days after
Chriſtmas, ſay,* as
was made very man, of the ſub-   *at this time.*
ſtance of the bleſſed Virgin Mary his mother,
and that without ſpot of ſin, to make us clean
from all ſin. Therefore with angels, &c.

¶ *Upon Eaſter-day, and ſeven days after.*

BUT chiefly are we bound to praiſe thee,
for the glorious reſurrection of thy Son
Jeſus Chriſt our Lord: For he is the very
Paſchal Lamb, which was offered for us, and
hath taken away the ſin of the world; who
by his death hath deſtroyed death, and by his
riſing to life again, hath reſtored to us everlaſting life. Therefore with angels, &c.

B   ¶ *Upon*

¶ *Upon Afcenfion-day, and feven days after.*

THROUGH thy moft dearly beloved Son, Jefus Chrift our Lord; who, after his moft glorious refurrection, manifeftly appeared to all his apoftles, and in their fight afcended up into heaven, to prepare a place for us; that where he is, thither might we alfo afcend, and reign with him in glory. Therefore with angels and archangels, &c.

¶ *Upon Whitfunday, and fix days after.*

THROUGH Jefus Chrift our Lord; according to whofe moft true promife the Holy Ghoft came down * [as on

* *During the fix days after Whitfunday, fay, as at this time.*

this day] from heaven, with a fudden great found, as it had been a mighty wind, in the likenefs of fiery tongues, lighting upon the apoftles, to teach them, and to lead them to all truth, giving them both the gift of divers languages, and alfo boldnefs with fervent zeal conftantly to preach the gofpel unto all nations, whereby we are brought out of darknefs and error into the clear light and true knowledge of thee, and of thy Son Jefus Chrift. Therefore with angels, &c.

¶ *Upon the feaft of Trinity only.*

WHO art one God, one Lord; not one only perfon, but three perfons in one fubftance. For that which we believe of the

glory

glory of the Father, the fame we believe of the Son, and of the Holy Ghoft, without any difference or inequality. Therefore with angels, *&c.*

¶ *After which prefaces fhall follow immediately this doxology.*

THEREFORE with angels and archangels, and with all the company of heaven, we laud and magnify thy glorious name, evermore praifing thee, and faying, Holy, holy, holy Lord God of hofts, heaven and earth are full of thy glory. Glory be to thee, O Lord moft high. *Amen.*

¶ *Then the Prieft ftanding at fuch a part of the holy table as he may with the moft eafe and decency ufe both his hands, and fhall fay the prayer of confecration, as followeth.*

ALL glory be to thee, Almighty God, our heavenly Father, for that thou of thy tender mercy didft give thy only Son Jefus Chrift to fuffer death upon the crofs for our redemption; who made there (by his one oblation of himfelf once offered) a full, perfect, and fufficient facrifice, oblation, and fatisfaction, for the fins of the whole world; and did inftitute, and in his holy gofpel command us to continue a perpetual memory of that his precious death and facrifice until his coming again. For, in the night that he was betrayed, (*a*) he took bread; and when he had given

(*a*) *Here the Prieft is to take the paten into his hands:*

thanks,

(b) And here to break the bread:

(c) And here to lay his hands upon all the bread.

(d) Here he is to take the cup into his hand:

(e) And here to lay his hand upon every veſſel (be it chalice or flagon) in which there is any wine to be conſecrated.

thanks, (b) he brake it, and gave to his diſciples, ſaying, Take, eat, (c) THIS IS MY BODY, which is given for you: DO this in remembrance of me. Likewiſe after ſupper (d) he took the cup; and when he had given thanks, he gave it to them, ſaying, Drink ye all of this, for (e) THIS IS MY BLOOD, of the new teſtament, which is ſhed for you, and for many, for the remiſſion of ſins: DO this as oft as ye ſhall drink it in remembrance of me.

The Oblation. WHerefore, O Lord, and heavenly Father, according to the inſtitution of thy dearly beloved Son our Saviour Jeſus Chriſt, we thy humble ſervants do celebrate and make here before thy divine majeſty, with theſe thy holy gifts, WHICH WE NOW OFFER UNTO THEE, the memorial thy Son hath commanded us to make; having in remembrance his bleſſed paſſion, and precious death, his mighty reſurrection, and glorious aſcenſion; rendering unto thee moſt hearty thanks for the innumerable benefits procured unto us by the

The Invocation. ſame. And we moſt humbly beſeech thee, O merciful Father, to hear us, and of thy almighty goodneſs nefs vouchfafe to blefs and fanctify, with thy word and Holy Spirit, thefe thy gifts and creatures of bread and wine, that they may become the body and blood of thy moft dearly beloved Son. And we earneftly defire thy fatherly goodnefs, mercifully to accept this our facrifice of praife and thankfgiving, moft humbly befeeching thee to grant, that by the merits and death of thy Son Jefus Chrift, and through faith in his blood, we (and all thy whole church) may obtain remiffion of our fins, and all other benefits of his paffion. And here we offer and prefent unto thee, O Lord, ourfelves, our fouls and bodies, to be a reafonable, holy and lively facrifice unto thee, humbly befeeching thee, that we and all others who fhall be partakers of this holy Communion, may worthily receive the moft precious body and blood of thy Son Jefus Chrift, be filled with thy grace and heavenly benediction, and made one body with him, that he may dwell in them and they in him. And although we are unworthy, through our manifold fins, to offer unto thee any facrifice; yet we befeech thee to accept this our bounden duty and fervice, not weighing our merits, but pardoning our offences, through Jefus Chrift our Lord: by whom, and with whom, in the unity of the Holy Ghoft, all honour and glory be unto thee, O Father Almighty, world without end. *Amen.*

C ¶ *Let*

¶ *Let us pray for the whole ſtate of Chriſt's Church.*

ALMIGHTY and everliving God, who by thy holy Apoſtle haſt taught us to make prayers and ſupplications, and to give thanks for all men; We humbly beseech thee moſt mercifully to accept our alms and oblations, and to receive theſe our prayers, which we offer unto thy divine majeſty; beſeeching thee to inſpire continually the univerſal church with the ſpirit of truth, unity and concord; and grant that all they who do confeſs thy holy name, may agree in the truth of thy holy word and live in unity and godly love. We beſeech thee also to ſave and defend all Chriſtian Kings, Princes, and Governors; and grant that they, and all who are in authority, may truly and impartially miniſter juſtice to the puniſhment of wickedneſs and vice, and to the maintenance of thy true religion and virtue. Give grace, O heavenly Father, to all Biſhops, Prieſts, and Deacons, that they may both by their life and doctrine ſet forth thy true and lively word, and rightly and duly adminiſter thy holy ſacraments: and to all thy people give thy heavenly grace, that with meek heart, and due reverence, they may hear and receive thy holy word, truly ſerving thee in holineſs and righteouſneſs all the days of their life. And we commend eſpecially to thy merciful goodneſs the congregation here
                                    aſſembled

affembled in thy name, to celebrate the commemoration of the moft precious death and facrifice of thy Son and our Saviour Jefus Chrift. And we moft humbly befeech thee of thy goodnefs, O Lord, to comfort and fuccour all thofe who in this tranfitory life are in trouble, forrow, need, ficknefs, or any other adverfity. And we alfo blefs thy holy name for all thy fervants, who, having finifhed their courfe in faith, do now reft from their labours: yielding unto thee moft high praife and hearty thanks, for the wonderful goodnefs and virtue declared in all thy faints, who have been the choice veffels of thy grace, and the lights of the world in their feveral generations: moft humbly befeeching thee to give us grace to follow the example of their ftedfaftnefs in thy faith, and obedience to thy holy commandments, that at the day of the general refurrection, we, and all they who are of the myftical body of thy Son, may be fet on his right hand, and hear that his moft joyful voice, Come, ye bleffed of my father, inherit the kingdom prepared for you from the foundation of the world. Grant this, O Father, for Jefus Chrift's fake, our only Mediator and Advocate. *Amen.*

As our Saviour Chrift hath commanded and taught us, we are bold to fay,

OUR Father who art in heaven, Hallowed be thy name. Thy kingdom come. Thy will be done in earth as it is in heaven. Give us this day our daily bread. And forgive us our trefpaffes, as we forgive them that trefpafs againſt us. And lead us not into temptation; but deliver us from evil. For thine is the kingdom, and the power and the glory, forever and ever. *Amen.*

¶ *Then ſhall the Prieſt ſay to them that come to receive the holy communion, this invitation.*

YE, that do truly and earneſtly repent you of your fins, and are in love and charity with your neighbours, and intend to lead a new life, following the commandments of God, and walking from henceforth in his holy ways: Draw near with faith and take this holy ſacrament to your comfort; and make your humble confeſſion to Almighty God.

¶ *Then ſhall this general confeſſion be made, by the people, along with the Prieſt; all humbly kneeling upon their knees.*

ALMIGHTY God, Father of our Lord Jeſus Chriſt, maker of all things, judge of all men; We acknowledge and bewail our manifold fins and wickedneſs, which we from time to time moſt grievioufly have committed, by thought, word, and deed, againſt thy divine Majeſty; provoking moſt juſtly thy wrath and indignation againſt us. We do earneſtly repent, and are heartily ſorry for theſe our miſdoings; the remembrance of them is grievous unto us; the burden of them

is

is intolerable. Have mercy upon us, have mercy upon us, moſt merciful Father; for thy Son our Lord Jeſus Chriſt's ſake, forgive us all that is paſt; and grant, that we may ever hereafter ſerve and pleaſe thee, in newneſs of life, to the honour and glory of thy name, through Jeſus Chriſt our Lord. *Amen.*

¶ *Then ſhall the Prieſt, or the Biſhop, (being preſent,) ſtand up, and turning himſelf to the people, pronounce the abſolution as followeth.*

ALmighty God our heavenly Father, who, of his great mercy, hath promiſed forgiveneſs of ſins to all them that with hearty repentance and true faith turn unto him; Have mercy upon you; pardon and deliver you from all your ſins; confirm and ſtrengthen you in all goodneſs; and bring you to everlaſting life, through Jeſus Chriſt our Lord. *Amen.*

¶ *Then ſhall the Prieſt ſay,*

Hear what comfortable words our Saviour Chriſt ſaith unto all that truly turn to him:

COME unto me, all ye that labour, and are heavy laden, and I will refreſh you. *Matth.* ix. 28.

Private ejaculation.
Refreſh, O Lord, thy ſervant wearied with the burden of ſin.

God so loved the world, that he gave his only begotten Son, that whoſoever believeth

in

in him, fhould not perifh, but have everlafting life. *John* iii. 16.

Private ejaculation.

*Lord, I believe in thy Son Jefus Chrift, and let this faith
purify me from all iniquity.*

Hear alfo what St. Paul faith.

This is a faithful faying, and worthy of
all acceptation, that Chrift Jefus came into
the world to fave finners. 1 *Tim.* i. 15.

Private ejaculation.

*I embrace with all thankfulnefs that falvation that Je-
fus has brought into the world.*

Hear alfo what St. John faith.

If any man fin, we have an advocate with
the Father, Jefus Chrift the righteous: and
he is the propitiation for our fins. 1 *John*
ii. 1, 2.

Private ejaculation.

*Intercede for me, O bleffed Jefu! that my fins may be
pardoned, through the merits of thy death.*

¶ *Then fhall the Prieft, turning him to the
altar, kneel down, and fay, in the name of
all them that fhall communicate, this collect
of humble accefs to the holy communion, as
followeth.*

WE do not prefume to come to this thy
holy table, O merciful Lord, trufting
in our own righteoufnefs, but in thy manifold and great mercies. We are not worthy
fo much as to gather up the crumbs under
thy table: But thou art the fame Lord, whofe
property is always to have mercy. Grant us
therefore, gracious Lord, fo to eat the flefh

of

of thy dear Son Jefus Chrift, and to drink his blood, that our finful bodies may be made clean by his moft facred body, and our fouls wafhed through his moft precious blood, and that we may evermore dwell in him, and he in us. *Amen.*

¶ *Then fhall the Bifhop, if he be prefent, or elfe the Prieft that celebrateth, firft receive the communion in both kinds himfelf, and next deliver it to other Bifhops, Prefbyters, and Deacons, (if there be any prefént,) and after to the people in due order, all humbly kneeling. And when he receiveth himfelf, or delivereth the facrament of the body of Chrift to others, he fhall fay,*

THE body of our Lord Jefus Chrift, which was given for thee, preferve thy foul and body unto everlafting life.

¶ *Here the perfon receiving fhall fay,* Amen.

¶ *And when the Prieft receiveth the cup himfelf, or delivereth it to others, he fhall fay,*

THE blood of our Lord Jefus Chrift, which was fhed for thee, preferve thy foul and body unto everlafting life.

¶ *Here the perfon receiving fhall fay,* Amen.

¶ *If the confecrated bread or wine be all fpent before all have communicated, the Prieft is to confecrate more, according to the form before prefcribed, beginning at the words,* All glory

glory be to thee, *&c. and ending with the words,* that they may become the body and blood of thy moſt dearly beloved Son.

¶ *When all have communicated, he that celebrates ſhall go to the Lord's table, and cover with a fair linen cloth that which remaineth of the conſecrated elements, and then ſay,*
Having

Private Devotions for the Altar.

BLESSED Jeſus! Saviour of the world! who haſt called me to the participation of theſe thy holy myſteries, accept my humble approach to thy ſacred table, increase my faith, ſettle my devotion, fix my contemplation on thy powerful mercy; and while with my mouth I receive the ſacred ſymbols of thy body and blood, may they be the means of heavenly nouriſhment to prepare my body and ſoul for that everlaſting life which thou haſt purchaſed by thy merits, and promiſed to beſtow on all who believe in and depend on thee. *Amen.*

Prayer to God.

O Gracious and merciful God, Thou ſupreme Being, Father, Word and Holy Ghoſt, look down from heaven, the throne of thy eſſential glory, upon me thy unworthy creature, with the eyes of thy covenanted mercy and compaſſion: O Lord my God, I diſclaim all merit, I renounce all righteouſneſs of my own, either inherent in my nature, or acquired by my own induſtry: And I fly for refuge, for pardon and ſactification, to the righteouſneſs of thy Chriſt: For his ſake, for the ſake of the bleſſed Jeſus, the Son of thy covenanted love, whom Thou haſt ſet forth to be a propitiation for fallen man, and in whom alone Thou art well pleaſed, have
mercy

Having now received the precious body and
blood of Chrift, let us give thanks to our
Lord God, who hath gracioufly vouchfa-
fed to admit us to the participation of his
holy myfteries; and let us beg of him grace
to perform our vows, and to perfevere in
our good refolutions; that being made holy,
we may obtain everlafting life, through the
merits of the all-fufficient facrifice of our
Lord and Saviour Jefus Chrift.

Then

---

mercy upon me, receive my prayers, pardon my infir-
mities, ftrengthen my weak refolutions, guide my fteps
to thy holy altar, and there feed me with the meat
which perifheth not, but endureth to everlafting life.
Amen.

After Receiving.

BLESSED Jefus! Thou haft now bleft me with the
food of thy own merciful inftitution, and, in humble faith of thy gracious promife, I have bowed myfelf
at thy table, to receive the precious pledges of thy dying love; O may thy prefence go with me from this
happy participation of thy goodnefs, that when I return
to the neceffary labours and employments of this miferable world, I may be enabled by thy grace to obey thy
commandments, and conducted by thy watchful care
through all trials, till, according to thy divine wifdom,
I have finifhed my courfe here with joy, that fo I may
depart out of this world in peace, and in a ftedfaft de-
pendence on thy merits, O blefled Jefus, in whofe pre-
vailing words I fhut up all my imperfect wifhes, faying,

Our Father, &c. Amen.

D

¶ *Then the Prieſt ſhall ſay this collect of thankſgiving, as followeth.*

ALMIGHTY and everliving God, we moſt heartily thank thee, for that thou doſt vouchſafe to feed us, who have duly received theſe holy myſteries, with the ſpiritual food of the moſt precious body and blood of thy Son our Saviour Jeſus Chriſt; and doth aſſure us thereby of thy favour and goodneſs towards us, and that we are very members incorporate in the myſtical body of thy Son, which is the bleſſed company of all faithful people, and are alſo heirs through hope of thy everlaſting kingdom, by the merits of his moſt precious death and paſſion. We now moſt humbly beſeech thee, O heavenly Father, ſo to aſſiſt us with thy grace and Holy Spirit, that we may continue in that holy communion and fellowſhip, and do all ſuch good works as thou haſt commanded us to walk in, through Jeſus Chriſt our Lord; to whom, with Thee and the Holy Ghoſt, be all honour and glory, world without end. *Amen.*

¶ *Then ſhall be ſaid or ſung,* Gloria in excelſis, *as followeth.*

GLORY be to God on high, and in earth peace, good will towards men. We praiſe thee, we bleſs thee, we worſhip thee, we glorify thee, we give thanks to thee, for thy great glory, O Lord God, heavenly King, God

God the Father Almighty; and to Thee, O God, the only begotten Son Jeſu Chriſt; and to Thee, O God, the Holy Ghoſt..

O Lord, the only begotten Son Jeſu Chriſt; O Lord God, Lamb of God, Son of the Father, who takeſt away the ſins of the world, have mercy upon us. Thou that takeſt away the ſins of the world, receive our prayer. Thou that ſitteſt at the right hand of God the Father, have mercy upon us.

For thou only art holy, thou only art the Lord, thou only, O Chriſt, with the Holy Ghoſt, art moſt high in the glory of God the Father. *Amen.*

¶ *Then the Prieſt, or Biſhop, if he be preſent, ſhall let them depart, with this bleſſing.*

THE peace of God, which paſſeth all underſtanding, keep your hearts and minds in the knowledge and love of God, and of his Son Jeſus Chriſt our Lord: and the bleſſing of God Almighty, the Father, the Son, and the Holy Ghoſt be amongſt you, and remain with you always. *Amen.*

THE END.

HISTORICAL SKETCH

AND NOTES.

HISTORICAL SKETCH.

On the twenty-third Sunday after Trinity, November 14th, 1784, at the chapel in Bishop Skinner's house in Longacre, Aberdeen, "in the presence of a considerable number of respectable clergymen, and a great number of laity," Dr. Samuel Seabury was consecrated Bishop of Connecticut, by the Rt. Rev. Messrs. Kilgour, Petrie, and Skinner, Bishops of the Episcopal Church in Scotland. On the following day a "Concordate" between the Church in Scotland and that in Connecticut was agreed upon, and signed and sealed by the four Bishops. Of this Concordate the fifth article is in the following words :

"Art. V. As the Celebration of the holy Eucharist, or the Administration of the Sacrament of the Body and Blood of Christ, is the principal Bond of Union among Christians, as well as the most solemn Act of Worship in the Christian Church, the Bishops aforesaid agree in desiring that there may be as little Variance here as possible ; and tho' the Scottish Bishops are very far from prescribing to their Brethren in this matter, they cannot help ardently wishing that Bishop Seabury would endeavour all he can, consistently with peace and prudence, to make the Celebration of this venerable Mystery conformable to the most primitive Doctrine and Practice in that respect: Which is the pattern the Church of Scotland has copied after in her Communion Office, and which it has been the Wish of some of the most eminent Divines of the Church of England, that she also had more closely followed than she seems

to have done since she gave up her first reformed Liturgy, used in
the Reign of King Edward VI., between which, and the form used
in the Church of Scotland, there is no Difference in any point,
which the primitive Church reckoned essential to the right Ministration of the holy Eucharist.   In this capital Article therefore of
the Eucharistic Service, in which the Scottish Bishops so earnestly
wish for as much Unity as possible, Bishop Seabury also agrees to
take a serious View of the Communion Office recommended by
them, and if found agreeable to the genuine Standards of Antiquity,
to give his Sanction to it, and by gentle Methods of Argument and
Persuasion, to endeavour, as they have done, to introduce it by de-
grees into practice, without the Compulsion of Authority on the
one side, or the prejudice of former Custom on the other."[1]

The clergy of Connecticut assembled in Convocation
at Middletown, on the 2d day of August, 1785, and
gave their Bishop a hearty welcome.   We are told that
when the Concordate, with the accompanying letter from
the Scotch Bishops, was laid before the clergy, it excited
in them the warmest sentiments of gratitude and esteem.[2]
At this meeting the Rev. Messrs. Bowden and Jarvis of
Connecticut and the Rev. Mr. Parker of Boston were
appointed a committee to act with the Bishop in propos-
ing such changes in the Prayer-Book as should be thought
needful.   The committee met immediately and agreed
upon certain alterations.   Part of these were reserved to
be reported to the next meeting of Convocation, which
was to be held at New Haven in September[3]; but the
changes in the state prayers were published at once by
the Bishop in the following pastoral letter:

---

[1] Fac-simile Publications of the Historical Club, No. 13.

[2] Dr. Beardsley's History of the Church in Connecticut, i. 368.

[3] Dr. Parker's letter in Documentary History of Conn., ii. 318.

SAMUEL, by divine permiffion, Bifhop of the Epifcopal Church in the State of Connecticut, to the Clergy of the faid Church, GREETING.

IT having pleafed Almighty GOD, that the late *Britifh* Colony of Connecti-cut fhould become a free, fovereign and independent State, as it now is, fome alterations in the Liturgy and Offices of our Church are neceffary to be made, to accommodate them to the civil Conftitution of the country in which we live; for the peace, fecurity and profperity of which, both as good fub-jects and faithful Chriftians, it is our duty conftantly to pray——WE, the Bifhop aforefaid, have thought fit, by and with the advice and affiftance of fuch of our Clergy as we have had opportunity of confulting, to iffue this *Injunction*, hereby authorifing and requiring You, and every one of You, the Prefbyters and Deacons of the Church above mentioned, in the celebra-tion of Divine Service, to make the following alterations in the Liturgy and Offices of our Church, *viz.*

I. In the fuffrages after the Creed, in morning and evening Prayer, inftead of *O Lord fave the King,* You are to read, *O Lord fave the Church*; to which the congregation are to make the accuftomed refponfe, *And mercifully hear us,* &c.

II. The prayer for the King, in the morning and evening fervice, to be left out; and the prayer for the Royal Family to be thus altered; *Almighty God, the fountain of all goodnefs, we humbly befeech thee to blefs the* Governor and Rulers *of this State; endue them with thy Holy Spirit;*—and fo on as it now ftands.

III. In the Litany the 15, 16, 17, 18th petitions to be omitted, and the petition for Bifhops, Priefts, and Deacons, immediately to follow that for the univerfal Church. The 20, and 21ft petitions to be thus read, *That it may pleafe thee to endue the* Governor and Rulers *of this State, with grace, wifdom and underftanding. That it may pleafe thee to blefs and keep the Judges and inferior Magiftrates, giving them grace to execute juftice and to maintain truth.* To both which the ufual refponfe---*We befeech thee to hear us, good Lord,---*is to be made by the congregation.

IV. In the prayer for the whole ftate of Chrift's Church, the part relating to Rulers and Minifters to be thus altered---*We befeech thee alfo to fave and defend all Chriftian Kings, Princes, and Governors; and grant that they, and all that are put in authority, may truly and impartially minifter juftice, to the punifhment of wickednefs and vice, and to the maintenance of true religion and virtue. Give grace, O heavenly Father, to all Bifhops, Priefts, and Deacons, that they may-* - -and fo on, as it now ftands.

V. The prayers for the King that ftand before the Nicene Creed in the Communion fervice, to be omitted.

VI. In the anfwer in the Catechifm to the queftion---What is thy duty towards thy neighbour? for---*to honor and obey the King*---fubftitute, *to hon-or and obey my civil Rulers, to fubmit myfelf,* &c.

3*

VII. That during every feffion of the Great and General Court, or Affembly, you do ufe the following collect, in its proper place, both in morning and evening prayer.

" Moft gracious God, we humbly befeech thee, as for this State in general, " fo efpecially for the great and general Court at this time affembled : That " thou wouldft be pleafed to direct and profper all their confultations to the " advancement of thy glory, the good of thy church, the fafety, honor, and " welfare of thy people ; that all things may be fo ordered and fettled by " their endeavours, upon the beft and fureft foundations, that peace and hap-" pinefs, truth and juftice, religion and piety may be eftablifhed among us " for all generations. Thefe and all other neceffaries for them, for us, and " thy whole church, we humbly beg in the name and mediation of Jefus " Chrift our moft bleffed Lord and Saviour. Amen.

VIII. That you difcontinue the obfervation of the fifth of November, the thirtieth of January, the twenty-ninth of May, and the twenty-fifth of October.

Commending you, Reverend Brethren, your congregations, and labours in the Gospel, to the grace, protection, and bleffing of Almighty God, We remain your affectionate brother and fervant in Chrift Jefus, our Lord.

Done at New-London,

Aug. 12th, 1785.

The Convention of Massachusetts, Rhode Island, and New Hampshire met at Boston, on the 7th of September, having before them the report of the committee appointed at Middletown in August. The changes in the state prayers were adopted, with the characteristic substitution of "Commonwealth" for "State," and recommended for immediate use. A considerable number of other alterations were also agreed to, but it was voted that their use should be postponed in order that it might be seen how far the other States would conform to them.[1] Dr. Parker, writing to Bishop Seabury on the 12th of September, says that this Convention adopted most of the changes proposed at Middletown, with a few others; the changes of any importance to which assent was not given, being expressly stated to be the

---

[1] Reprint of Mass. Journals, pp. 8, sqq.

omission of the second Lesson in the Morning Service, and that of the Gospel and the Exhortation in the Baptismal-Office.[1]   In the lack of records of the early Convocations of Connecticut, we look to the journal of the Massachusetts Convention for an account of suggested alterations ; and it is noticeable that the only changes proposed in the Communion-Office were the omission of the Lord's Prayer at the beginning, the omission of the prayers for the King, a different petition for rulers in the prayer for the Church Militant, somewhat different phraseology in the first Warning and the first Exhortation, and a permission to repeat the sentences at administration but once for all then present at the altar.[2]   It is evident, therefore, that Bishop Seabury took no steps in 1785 to introduce the Scotch Liturgy.   The Massachusetts Convention was kept under adjournments until, July 20th, 1786, and at last it was left to the discretion of the different parishes to adopt the alterations or to retain the old liturgy.[3]

Bishop Seabury sent a copy of the substitutes for the state prayers to Dr. (afterwards Bishop) White, of Philadelphia, under date of August 19, 1785, with the words: "Should more be done, it must be a work of time and great deliberation."[4]   And in fact, the clergy of Connecticut were found unwilling to agree to any other alterations in the Prayer-Book.   Especially when the convention of the states to the south of New England met

---

[1] Doc. Hist. Conn., ii. 284.

[2] Reprint of Mass. Journals, pp. 11, 12.

[3] Doc. Hist. Conn., ii. 319.

[4] Ibid., ii. 282.

at Philadelphia, September 27th to October 7th, 1785, and prepared the book since known as the " Proposed Book," the Churchmen of Connecticut were alarmed. Mr. Parker had hoped that the meeting at Philadelphia would go no further than his own convention had gone ; but he evidently felt aggrieved that the clergy of Connecticut were not willing to go so far. Bishop Seabury wrote to him, November 28th, 1785, as follows :

"Between the time of our parting at Middletown and the clerical meeting at New Haven, it was found that the Church people in Connecticut were much alarmed at the thoughts of any considerable alterations being made in the Prayer Book ; and upon the whole, it was judged best that no alterations should be attempted at present, but to wait till a little time shall have cooled down the tempers and conciliated the affections of people to each other. And since the convention at Philadelphia, which, as report says, has abrogated two creeds and nineteen articles, and taken great liberties with the prayers, &c., we are more apprehensive of proceeding to any alterations."[1]

This Proposed Book was published in the spring of 1786.[2] On the 22nd of September in the same year, Bishop Seabury delivered his second charge to his clergy assembled in Convocation at Derby. In it he said :

"It is always a disagreeable task to be obliged to mention any matter with censure, or even disapprobation ; and I am very happy that the measure of which I am now to take notice can call for animadversion only by way of caution. A number of Clergy and Laity in the southern States have undertaken to revise and alter the Liturgy and Offices and Government of the Church, and have exhibited a Prayer-book to the public. The time will not permit me to

[1] Ibid., ii. 287.
[2] The Prothonotary's certificate is dated April 1st, 1786.

say anything of the merit of the alterations in the Liturgy; but, I am persuaded, by an unprejudiced mind, some of them will be thought for the worse, most of them not for the better. But the authority on which they have acted is unknown in the Episcopal Church. The government of the Church by Bishops we hold to have been established by the Apostles, acting under the commission of Christ and the direction of the Holy Ghost; and therefore is not to be altered by any power on earth, nor indeed by an angel from heaven. This government they have degraded by lodging the chief authority in a Convention of clerical and lay Delegates, making their Church Episcopal in its orders, but Presbyterian in its government.

"Liturgies are left more to the prudence and judgment of the governors of the Church; and the primitive practice seems to have been that the Bishop did, with the advice no doubt of his Presbyters, provide a Liturgy for the use of his diocess. This ought to have been the case here. Bishops should first have been obtained to preside over those Churches. And to those Bishops, with the Proctors of the Clergy, should have been committed the business of compiling a Liturgy for the use of the Church throughout the states. This would have ensured unity in doctrine, worship, and discipline through the whole, which upon the present plan will either not be obtained, or, if obtained, will not be durable. And should we ever be so happy, through the merciful providence of God, as to obtain such a meeting, great regard ought to be had to the primitive Liturgies and Forms, in compiling a book of Common-Prayer."[1]

At this Convocation, Bishop Seabury, acting on the principles which he had thus laid down, set forth the Communion-Office which is reprinted in the foregoing pages, and "recommended" it "to the Episcopal Con-

---

[1] Pages 11, 12. The Bishop passes on to speak of the value of the testimony of the early Church, of the doctrine of the Sacraments, and of the necessity, in view of present dangers and errors, of holding fast to the primitive faith.

gregations in Connecticut."[1]   This office was taken, with
certain alterations which will presently be noticed in de-
tail, from that which was then in use in the Scotch
Church.   This latter is said to have been compiled by
Bishops Forbes and Falconer, and was first published in
1764.   Hall says that it "may be considered as the second
standard edition"; the first having been Bishop Gadderer's edition of 1743, which was recognized by the
canons of that year,[2] as the edition of 1764 (reprinted
in 1765) was by later canons.[3]

The first Scotch Prayer-Book was that published in
1637, under the direction of King Charles I.[4]   It is

---

[1] Dr. Jarvis's A Voice from Connecticut, p. 25; Dr. Beardsley's
Life of Bishop Seabury, p. 263.   A new State prayer was also provided. Ibid., p. 264.   The manuscript records of Convocation do not
begin till 1790, when the secretary was directed to procure a blank-
book in which to record the minutes.   Space was left at the beginning of the book as if to insert the minutes of former meetings,
but this was never done.   It seems, from a letter of the Rev.
Roger Viets of Simsbury to the Rev. Mr. Parker of Boston, that
the Convocation which met at Wallingford on the 27th of February
in the next year (1787) took steps towards setting forth for the use
of the Church in Connecticut a complete edition of the Prayer-
Book.   It was at this Convocation that a Coadjutor was elected to
Bishop Seabury; but the union of the dioceses in the country made
his consecration unnecessary.

[2] Fragmenta Liturgica, i., pp. liii., lv.   The "Non-juring" and
Scotch offices are in vol. v.

[3] Neale's Life of Torry, p. 270.   The edition of 1743 differs in
date only from that of 1735.

[4] His father King James (VI. of Scotland and I. of England)
had taken steps for composing a Scotch liturgy as early as 1616.
Sprott, Scottish Liturgies, p. xviii.

frequently called by the name of Archbishop Laud, who was appointed, together with Bishops Juxon and Wren, to examine and revise a draft which had been prepared in Scotland, the chief compilers being Maxwell, Bishop of Ross, and Wedderburn of Dunblane.[1] The chief variations from the English book which was then in use (that of 1559) were in the Communion-Office. The prayer for the Church Militant and the prayer of Consecration were more nearly conformed to the first book of Edward VI. than to that of Elizabeth, the words of Institution being preceded by an Invocation and followed by an Oblation, an Intercession, and the Lord's Prayer. The words at the delivery of the elements were also the same as in 1549. The only variation in *order* between the proposed Scotch liturgy and that then in use in England, was that the prayer of Humble Access was placed after the prayer of Consecration.

The Prayer-Book of 1637, as is well known, was at once withdrawn; but the subsequent Scotch Communion-Offices were to some extent modelled upon that contained in it. Changes, however, began to be made in the order of the several parts of the service; and in 1735 Gadderer's book appeared, having the order which was contained in the book of 1764 and in Bishop Seabury's office, except that the Offertory preceded the Ex-

---

[1] Sprott, ibid., Introduction, to page lxv.; Skinner on the Scotch Communion-Office (Aberdeen, 1807), p. 25; Hall, Reliquiæ Liturgicæ, i., pp. xix, sqq.; Bright in Blunt's Annotated P. B., pp. 580, sqq. Bp. Juxon took no part in the revision; but Bp. Cosin would seem to have been concerned in it; see Sprott, lix., note i.

hortation, and that, in the prayer of Consecration, the Invocation preceded the words of Institution. The words of Institution, the Oblation, and the Invocation had appeared in this their primitive and true order, for the first time in any service-book in the English language, in Stephens's "Liturgy of the Ancient Christians," about the year 1700[1]; and this order is found also in the Non-Jurors' book of 1718, in Deacon's Liturgy of 1734, in Rattray's of 1744, and in a Scotch office of 1755, to which that of 1764 is in every respect in close resemblance.[2]

The following collation shows the changes which Bishop Seabury introduced into the Scotch office of 1764. Every difference in words has been noted; only unimportant changes in punctuation and in the use of capitals have been omitted.

Page. line.	*Scotch Office*, 1764.	*Bishop Seabury's*, 1786.
3, 7	what St. Paul writeth to the Corinthians; how he exhorteth	how St. Paul exhorteth
17	unworthily. For then we are guilty of the body and blood of Christ our Saviour: we eat and drink our own damnation, not considering the Lord's body: we kindle God's wrath against us; we provoke him to plague us with divers diseases, and sundry kinds of death.	unworthily, not considering the Lord's body; for then we are guilty of the body and blood of Christ our Saviour; we kindle God's wrath against us, and bring his judgments upon us.

---

[1] Frag. Liturg., ii. 61, sqq.

[2] The Non-Jurors' and Scotch services may be found in Frag. Liturg., vol. v., Deacon's in vol. vi., and Rattray's in vol. i. See Neale's Life of Torry, chap. vii.

Page.line.		*Scotch Office,* 1764.	*Bishop Seabury's,* 1786.
3,	23	Lord. Repent you	Lord ; repent you
4,	5	humble	most humble
5,	1	*Presbyter*	*Priest*
		[and so throughout.]	
	6	*by his discretion, according to the length or shortness of the time that the people are offering.*	*in his discretion.*
	10	Lord : and Abel,	Lord. And Abel,
6,	22	charges ? Who planteth	charges ? who planteth
	27	a great thing if we shall	a great matter if we should
	30	live of the things of the temple ?	live of the sacrifice ?
7,	4	He who soweth	He that soweth
8,	5	*people there present*	*people*
	7	*bring the said bason with the oblations therein, and deliver it*	*bring, and deliver it*
	20	*upon the Lord's Table ; and shall say,*	*upon the Lord's table, putting a little pure water into the cup : and shall say,*
11,	12	Amen.	*Amen.*
	15	*both his hands, shall say*	*both his hands, and[1] shall say,*
	21	who (by his own oblation of himself once offered) made a full,	who made there (by his one oblation of himself once offered) a full,
	26	a perpetual memorial	a perpetual memory
13,	15	beseeching thee, that whosoever shall be partakers	humbly beseeching thee, that we and all others who shall be partakers
	19	and be filled	be filled
14,	7	our alms,	our alms and oblations,
	16	and especially thy servant our King, that under him we may be godly and quietly governed. And grant unto his whole Council, and to all who are put in authority under him, that they may truly and indifferently administer justice,	and grant that they, and all who are in authority, may truly and impartially administer justice

---

[1] Evidently a misprint.

Page. line.	*Scotch Office*, 1764.	*Bishop Seabury's*, 1786.
14, 31	which is here assembled	here assembled
15, 10	labours. And we yield unto thee	labours : yielding unto thee
12	wonderful grace and virtue	wonderful goodness and virtue
27	¶ *Then shall the Presbyter say :*	[No rubric.]
16, 7	*Then the Presbyter shall say*	*Then shall the Priest say*
14	Draw near, and take	Draw near with faith and take
18	*with the Presbyter ; he first kneeling down.*	*with the Priest ; all humbly kneeling upon their knees.*
17, 14	all them who	all them that
21	*Then shall the Presbyter also say,*	*Then shall the Priest say,*
25	I will give you rest. [No " Private Ejaculations " or " Private Devotions for the Altar."]	I will refresh you.
19, 4	our souls washed	and our souls washed
20	*And the Presbyter, or Minister, that receiveth the cup himself, or delivereth it to others, shall say this Benediction :*	*And when the Priest receiveth the cup himself, or delivereth it to others, he shall say,*
21, 7	resolutions ; and that, being	resolutions ; that being
22, 8	and dost assure us	and doth[1] assure us
21	with the Father, and	with Thee and
26	to God in the highest,	to God on high,

It may be of interest to add that the Scotch Communion-Office has remained almost without change since 1764. The edition published by the Rev. John Skinner of Forfar (son of the Bishop of Aberdeen), in 1800,[2] and reprinted by him in his " Scotch Communion-Office Illustrated," in 1807, differs from it only in the

---

[1] Evidently a misprint.

[2] Hall calls it the third standard edition. It may be found in Frag. Liturg., v. 253.

insertion of the words " and oblations " and the name of
the Sovereign in the prayer for the Church, the change
of " who " into " which " in the Lord's Prayer, the addition of " meekly kneeling upon your knees " to the
Invitation, the insertion of "and " before " our souls "
in the prayer of Humble Access, and the change of
" soul and body " into "body and soul " in the words of
administration. Bishop Torry's Prayer-Book, published
in Edinburgh in 1849,[1] besides prefixing an "Ante-Communion Service " (of which more will be said presently),
makes the same changes except that in the Invitation,
begins a new paragraph in the Trisagion at the word
" Holy," and does the same in the Prayer of Consecration at the beginning of the Invocation and of each of the
two following petitions. As at present printed for use,
the Scotch Communion-Office prefixes an " Ante-Communion Service," and agrees in other respects with the
edition of 1800 and 1807, except that the Trisagion is
printed in two paragraphs, the prayer of Consecration in
nine, and the prayer for the Church in nine.

Although the old Scotch Communion-Offices begin
with the Exhortation, we have the testimony of Mr.
Skinner in a note to Bishop Horsley's Collation of Offices, which forms an appendix to his " Scotch Communion-Office Illustrated," that an introductory service was
used; and the form which is given agrees substantially
with that in the two services mentioned at the end of the
last paragraph. This latter form differs from that in the

---

[1] The history of this book should be read in Neale's Life of
Bishop Torry, chaps. vii. and viii.; in the appendix to which it is
collated with the book of 1637, the Non-Jurors' office, and the
received Scotch form (that of 1764).

English book in allowing our Lord's summary of the Law
followed by a versicle to be read instead of the Ten Commandments with their versicles; in providing the collect
for grace and strength to keep the Commandments, its
use being discretionary with one of the two collects for the
Sovereign; and in instructing the people to say when the
Gospel is announced, " Glory be to Thee, O God," and
at its end, " Thanks be to Thee, O Lord, for this Thy
glorious Gospel."[1]   It is probable that Bishop Seabury
and his clergy used the " Ante-Communion Service " of
the English Book; for in a folio English Prayer-Book
which was used by the Bishop in St. James's Church,
New London, after the Revolution, is our present prayer
for the civil authority, written out and pasted over the
prayer for the Sovereign which follows the Commandments.[2]

Bishop Seabury's Communion-Office seems to have
been almost, if not quite, universally adopted by the
clergy of Connecticut. We are told that they " became
very much attached to it, not only from the recommend-

---

[1] Bishop Torry's edition, following that of 1637, directs the
Priest to say, " Here endeth the Holy Gospel "; but there is no
such direction in the later edition.   There were two sets of
rubrics in 1637, one in the usual place, and the other before and
after the Gospel for the First Sunday in Advent.

[2] Dr. Hallam's Annals of St. James's Church, p. 72. The first
Church in New London was burned in 1781, and the second was
not finished till 1787. There is a tradition that, while Bishop
Seabury officiated in the Court-House, he celebrated the Holy Communion every Sunday after morning prayer, in the large parlor of
the house in which he lived. Ibid., p. 71. He would naturally
begin with the Exhortation. See below.

ation of their Bishop, but from the conviction that this order was in more exact conformity [than the English liturgy] with the earliest usage of the Christian Church."[1] Its general use probably ceased when the American Book of Common Prayer began to be used, October 1st, 1790; but, as will be noted below, it was employed by some of the clergy at a much later date.

A "General Convention" assembled at Philadelphia, July 28th, 1789. On the 5th day of August, on motion of the Rev. Dr. William Smith of Maryland, it was voted (*inter alia*) that "it be proposed to the churches in the New England states to meet the churches of these states, with the said three Bishops [the Rt. Rev. Drs. White, Provoost, and Seabury], in an adjourned Convention, to settle certain articles of union among all the churches."[2] The clergy of Connecticut met on the 15th of September, and on the next day they elected the Rev. Messrs. Hubbard and Jarvis their delegates to the adjourned convention. They were "empowered to confer with the General Convention on the subject of making alterations in the Book of Common Prayer; but the ratification of such alterations was expressly reserved, to rest with the Bishop and clergy of the Church."[3] The Convention assembled on the 29th of September, and it was divided into two houses on the 3d of October. One of the first votes of the House of Clerical and Lay Deputies ordered the appointment of a committee "to prepare an order for the administration of the Holy Communion." This committee reported on the 9th, one day after the House

---

[1] Dr. Beardsley's History, i. 388. [2] Journal, p. 14.
[3] Beardsley, i. 409, 410.

4*

of Bishops (the Rt. Rev. Drs. Seabury and White) had "prepared their proposals" on this service. On the 13th, the lower house agreed to the report of their committee on the Communion Service; and on the 14th, the proposed service was sent to the Bishops, who at once made amendments and returned it. The lower house concurred in all the amendments except one, which was immediately withdrawn by the Bishops; and thus both houses agreed to the present American Communion-Office on the 14th day of October, 1789.[1]

That it was owing to Bishop Seabury that the Prayer of Consecration in that office followed the Scotch model is beyond a question. In a letter which he wrote to Bishop White, under date of June 29, 1789, after criticizing the action of the Philadelphia Convention in other matters, he had written as follows:

"That the most exceptionable part of the English book is the Communion Office may be proved by a number of very respectable names among her Clergy. The grand fault in that office is the deficiency of a more formal oblation of the elements, and of the invocation of the Holy Ghost to sanctify and bless them. The Consecration is made to consist merely in the Priest's laying his hands on the elements and pronouncing 'This is my body,' &c., which words are not consecration at all, nor were they addressed by Christ to the Father, but were declarative to the Apostles. This is so exactly symbolizing with the Church of Rome in an error; an error, too, on which the absurdity of Transubstantiation is built, that nothing but having fallen into the same error themselves, could have prevented the enemies of the Church from casting it in her teeth. The efficacy of Baptism, of Confirmation, of Orders, is ascribed to the Holy Ghost, and His energy is implored for that purpose; and why He

---

[1] Journal of Convention.

should not be invoked in the consecration of the Eucharist, especially as all the old Liturgies are full to the point, I cannot conceive. It is much easier to account for the alterations of the first Liturgy of Edward the VI., than to justify them; and as I have been told there is a vote on the minutes of your Convention, anno 1786, I believe, for the revision of this matter, I hope it will be taken up, and that God will raise up some able and worthy advocate for this primitive practice, and make you and the Convention the instruments of restoring it to His Church in America. It would do you more honor in the world, and contribute more to the union of the churches than any other alterations you can make, and would restore the Holy Eucharist to its ancient dignity and efficacy."[1]

The strength of Bishop Seabury's convictions on this subject appeared when, on the morning of Sunday, the 11th of October, during the session of the Convention, Bishop White asked him to consecrate the elements, and he twice declined, saying the second time in a pleasant manner: " To confess the truth, I hardly consider the form to be used [that of the English book] as strictly amounting to a consecration."[2]

" It may perhaps be expected," says Bishop White, "that the great change made in restoring to the consecration prayer the oblatory words and the invocation of the Holy Spirit, left out in King Edward's reign, must at least have produced an opposition. But no such thing

---

[1] Doc. Hist. Conn., ii. 331. See also Bp. Seabury's Sermon " Of the Holy Eucharist " (Sermons, Vol. i., Discourse vi.), in which reference is made to Brett's Dissertation and to [Bp. Rattray's] Liturgy of Jerusalem.

[2] Bp. White's Memoirs of the Church, second edition, pp. 154, 155. " These sentiments he had adopted," adds Bp. White, " in his visit to the bishops from whom he received his Episcopacy." This, though at first sight a natural supposition, is probably a mistake.

happened to any considerable extent; or at least, the author did not hear of any in the other house, further than
a disposition to the effect in a few gentlemen, which was
counteracted by some pertinent remarks of the president.
In that of the bishops, it lay very near to the heart of
Bishop Seabury. As for the other bishop [Bishop White
himself], without conceiving with some, that the service
as it stood was essentially defective, he always thought
there was a beauty in those ancient forms, and can dis-
cover no superstition in them."[1] He then goes on to
explain how in the first edition of the new book the words
"which we now offer unto thee" were printed, as in the
Scotch office, in small capitals; though in all succeeding
editions[2] they were, as was intended, in the same type as
the rest of the prayer.

The president of the lower house, whose pertinent remarks are said by Bishop White to have counteracted
some disposition to raise objections to the change proposed, was the Rev. Dr. William Smith, who has been
mentioned above. Dr. Smith was a native of Scotland,
who had been ordained to the diaconate and the priest-
hood at the same time and place as Bishop Seabury. On
grounds which need not be mentioned here, he "had

---

[1] Ibid., p. 154.

[2] This is not quite accurate. The small capitals appear in the
editions of both 1790 and 1791. Rev. Frederick Gibson's Historical Essay, p. 23. In the first edition of the Prayer-Book, the
words in the Apostles' Creed, "He descended into hell," are en-
closed in brackets; but it is only in Evening Prayer that they are
printed in italics; in Morning Prayer and the Visitation of the
Sick they are in ordinary type. Bp. White's statement (Memoirs,
p. 151) needs this correction.

been opposed to the non-juring bishops in Scotland communicating the Episcopate to Connecticut; and he had said some things not very complimentary to the candidate from this State, in his steps to reach the apostolic office."[1] But, as we have seen, he had proposed the invitation to the Bishop and Clergy of Connecticut; he entertained the Bishop during his stay in Philadelphia; and tradition has it that, when certain members of the lower house were beginning to object to the prayer of Consecration which was proposed by the Bishops, he reproved them for finding fault with something which they had not heard, and thereupon read the prayer with so impressive a tone and manner that the objections were no further urged. The form, says Dr. Jarvis, "was admitted without opposition, and in silence if not in reverence."[2] It is, then, to Bishop Seabury and Dr. Smith that the Church in this country is indebted for its prayer of Consecration in the Communion-Office.

It was probably owing to the influence of the delegation from Maryland that the wording of the Invocation was changed from that in the Scotch office to that which we now use. Writing to the Rev. Mr. Parker of Boston, April 17th, 1786, Dr. Smith says that the Maryland Convention, having the " Proposed Book " under consideration, had decided to recommend "an addition to the Consecration Prayer, in the Holy Communion, something analogous to that of the Liturgy of Edward VI. and the Scots' Liturgy, invoking a blessing on the Elements of Bread and Wine," changing the prayer "that they may

---

[1] Beardsley, i. 377. Dr. Smith was at one time Provost of the University of Pennsylvania.

[2] A Voice from Connecticut, p. 26.

become the body and blood, etc." to " that we receiving the same, according to Thy Son, our Saviour Jesus Christ's holy Institution, etc." He adds: " This I think will be a proper amendment, and it perfectly satisfies such of our Clergy and people as were attached to the Scots' and other ancient Liturgies, all of which have an Invocation of a blessing on the Elements, as is, indeed, most proper."[1]

It may be worth while to note that both the Concordate quoted at the beginning of this sketch, and Bishop Seabury's letter, as well as Bishop White's words in his Memoirs, seem to imply that, in the opinion of the writers, the first Liturgy of Edward VI. and the Scotch office contained prayers of Consecration which were substantially the same; whereas in fact the Invocation in the first Book of Edward VI. stands in an anomalous place, followed as it is by the words of Institution, and that by

---

[1] Doc. Hist. Conn., i. 291. The vote of the Convention is printed in the appendix to the Journal of Maryland, 1855, p. 18. It is very interesting to note that the latter part of this form had been proposed in the draft of a Prayer-Book made in Scotland in the reign of King James (probably in 1619) and sent to London not later than 1629. Sprott, pp. xxxiv., lxx., 72. The prayer of Invocation, says this author, " is thought essential by the [Presbyterian] Church of Scotland, and to this day the want of it in the English Prayer-Book is spoken of among us as a very serious defect." Ibid., p. lxviii. Dr. Sancroft proposed a form almost identical with that adopted in 1789. Bulley's Variations, p. 191. Both phrases were used in 1637, the first having the form " that they may be unto us the body and bloud of Thy most dearly beloved Son." The Rev. William Smith of Stepney Parish, Md., as appears from a letter written in 1785, was in the habit of using the Scotch office, and persisted in it in spite of the objections of Dr. William Smith.

the Oblation; while in the Scotch Book the order is that
of the ancient Liturgies, as was noted above. Its compilers used the words of the book of 1549, but they put
them in the order which they knew to have the sanction
of antiquity.

Such was the great point in which Bishop Seabury's
liturgy influenced the formation of the Communion-Office
which is still, by God's good providence, used throughout the Church in the United States. It is thought that
this influence may be traced in another matter which,
though it is by no means of equal importance, is yet
worthy of careful consideration.

In the first Prayer-Book of King Edward VI., it was
provided that if the sermon did not contain an exhortation to the people " to the worthy receiving of the holy
Sacrament of the body and blood of our Saviour Christ,"
the curate should give an exhortation to those that were
minded to receive the same; and this exhortation, which
is nearly word for word the same that is still used in the
Communion Service, beginning "Dearly beloved in the
Lord," was followed by the Offertory. Then, if there was
no Communion, the Priest was instructed to say one or
two collects and to dismiss the people with the accustomed
blessing. But if there was a Communion, it was ordered
that those who intended to partake of it should " tarry
still in the quire or in some convenient place nigh the
quire," and that all others should " depart out of the
quire except the Ministers and Clerks." The prayer for
the Church, it may be noted, came after the Trisagion.
In 1552 the prayer for the Church was placed immediately after the Offertory, and the Minister was in-

structed, when there was no Communion, to say "all that
is appointed at the Communion till the end of the homily, concluding with the general prayer for the whole
estate of Christ's Church militant here in earth, and one
or more collects." The same rubric was repeated in
1559 and in 1604; in 1662 it was made more explicit,
requiring that everything should be said to the end of the
general prayer, and that the Blessing should be given
after the Collects. It was at this point in the service,
then, that non-communicants were expected to withdraw
from the Church.[1] But in the Non-jurors' Book of
1718, the Offertory is placed after the Exhortation,
which is addressed to the communicants, and is closely
followed, as in the later Scotch services, by the Trisagion; and at the end of the service, there is the following important rubric : "After the Sermon or Homily is
ended, (or, if there be no Sermon or Homily, after the
Nicene Creed is ended,) if there be no Communion, the
Priest shall turn to the people, and say, *Let us pray.*
And then, turning to the Altar, he shall stand before it,
and say one or more of these Collects last before re-
hearsed, concluding with the Blessing." The other
Scotch offices which are reprinted in Hall's Fragmenta
Liturgica contain no part of the service to be used before
the Sermon, and give no instructions as to what shall be
done when there is no Communion, it being evidently
considered that all that is printed is, as is expressly said
on the title-pages, the Communion-office " as far as con-
cerneth the Ministration of that Holy Sacrament." The

---

[1] See Scudamore, Notitia Eucharistica, first edition, p. 391, and
note the reference to Bp. Cosin.

editions of 1724 and 1743 begin with the Offertory; but that of 1755[1] and all that follow begin with the Exhortation; and on the reverse of the title-page of the edition of 1844, we find: "The Catechumens and other Non-Communicants being dismissed, the Holy Office proceedeth as here set forth." Bishop Torry's Prayer-Book has this rubric: "Then shall follow the Sermon; and when the Holy Eucharist is to be celebrated, the Minister shall dismiss the non-communicants in these or like words, *Let those who are not to communicate now depart.*" It would appear, then, as well from express directions in books which Bishop Seabury followed or which were based on those that he followed, as from the structure of the office which he set forth, that none but communicants were supposed to be present at the time of the Offertory; and if not at that time, then certainly not at the offering of the prayer for the Church, which invariably occupies a later place in the service.[2]

Now bearing these facts in mind, it certainly seems that the changes introduced in 1789 into certain of the rubrics of the English Liturgy, in adapting them to the use of the American Church, show that it was the intention of

---

[1] See the " Direction " on the reverse of the title.

[2] It ought perhaps to be noted that Bishop Drummond's service (1796) contemplates an offertory and the use of the prayer for the Church, and Bishop Torry's book (1849) an offertory, on occasions when there is no Communion. In the use of the prayer for the Church in the former service, it is curious to observe, the words " alms and " " are to be omitted, except when the offering is to be given away in charity. . . . N. B. The offerings of the people, when for the support of the clergy, are not *alms*, but *a debt*. See 1 Cor. ix. chap. from the 7. to the 15 verse."

the revisers that the non-communicants should withdraw
from the Church after the Sermon and before the
Offertory and the prayer for the Church.   The English
Book says: "Then shall follow the Sermon"—"Then
shall the Priest return to the Lord's Table and begin
the Offertory"—"And *when there is a Communion,* the
Priest shall then place upon the Table so much Bread
and Wine as he shall think sufficient."   But the American Book says: "Then shall follow the Sermon.   After
which, the Minister, *when there is a Communion,* shall
return to the Lord's Table and begin the Offertory"—
"And the Priest shall then place upon the Table so
much Bread and Wine as he shall think sufficient."
And instead of putting the break in the service at the
end of the prayer for the Church, the American Book
directs that when there is no Communion, there "shall
be said all that is appointed at the Communion, unto the
end of the Gospel, concluding with the Blessing."[1]

There can be no question as to the custom which pre-
vailed, in Connecticut at least, until twenty or twenty-
five years ago, when, in spite of tradition and the implied
direction of rubrics, the English custom began to be ob-
served.   The Convocation of the clergy of Connecticut,
at their meeting, September 6, 1821, resolved, "That
the congregations be dismissed, previous to the Communion service, with a Collect and the shorter benediction."[2]
This was done after the sermon, and the offerings were
received from communicants alone.   This was in accord-
ance with primitive usage; "for in these days it was a

---

[1] See also the last rubric in the Form of Consecration of a Church.
[2] Ms. Records.

privilege to be allowed to make their oblations, and a sort of lesser excommunication to be debarred from it " ; [1] and the great Intercession belonged to the most solemn part of the service.

Having thus used his influence successfully to secure to the Church in America a Communion-Office based on primitive models, and having more than fulfilled the requirements of the Concordate into which he had entered at the time of his consecration, Bishop Seabury returned to his Diocese. His clergy met in Convocation, June 2d, 1790, and made a " short examination " of the Constitution and Canons adopted at Philadelphia; but there is no minute on record of any action in regard to the Prayer-Book. An adjourned meeting was held at Newtown, September 30th, 1790, and on the second day of the session, October 1st, the very day on which the new book was to go into use, we find the following record made :

" The alterations in the Book of Common Prayer made by the General Convention at Philadelphia, were read and considered.

" On motion, The question was put, in these words : ' Whether we confirm the doings of our Proctors in the General Convention at Philadelphia, on the 2d day of Octob', 1789.'

" Which passed in the affirmative by the votes of every member present, the Rev'd Mr. Sayre excepted."[2]

On the following day

" A motion was made, that the Convocation should determine on a mode of introducing the Constitution & Canons & Liturgy in our several parishes : When it was agreed that each of the Clergy

---

[1] Bingham, Antiq., Book xv., chap. ii., § 2; vol. v., p. 197, ed. 1829.
[2] Ms. Records.

should take that method that should appear to him the most eligible. Agreed also that in the use of the New-Prayer-Book, we be as uniform as possible,—& for that purpose, that we approach as near the *Old Liturgy*, as a compliance with the Rubrics of the *New* will allow."[1]

On October 5th, 1791, it was

"Voted: That, in the use of the Common Prayer Book we will use the *Nicene-Creed* on Communion Days, and the Apostle's Creed on all other days."[2]

The new Prayer-Book having been thus adopted, "Bishop Seabury's office passed at once out of *general* use."[3] "But the change from established customs is seldom easy, and whether the people loved to have it so or not, some of the clergy of that day never learned to carry out in full practice the literal meaning of the rubrical directions of the new Prayer-Book."[4] Dr. Hallam says that the Rev. Charles Seabury (the Bishop's son, and his successor at New London, 1796–1814), probably used it, but that it was never used there after he himself became a communicant.[5] When he took charge of the parish in 1835, Dr. Hallam found some half dozen copies of the pamphlet lying about in the pews of the Church,[6] and it was from one of these, and through his kindness, that this reprint was made in 1874. The writer was informed by the late Rev. Dr. Haight, that Bishop Brownell told him that when he came into the Diocese in 1819, he found some of the older clergy still using Bishop Seabury's Communion-Office, and that he had considerable difficulty in persuading them to substitute the Prayer-Book office in its place.

---

[1] Ibid.   [2] Ibid.   [3] Dr. Beardsley.   [4] Id., Hist., i. 415.
[5] Ms. Letter.   [6] Annals, p. 71.

The latest remnant of the former use of which the writer has been able to learn was at Cheshire in 1835, when the Rev. Reuben Ives, a former rector of the parish, who had been ordained by Bishop Seabury and had been his assistant at New London, being called upon by the Rev. Dr. Beardsley, then a Deacon in charge of the Parish, to officiate in the Communion Service, "invariably read what is called the prayer of Humble Access immediately after consecrating the elements and just before communicating, as it stands at present in the Scottish office." [1]

So Bishop Seabury's office passed out of use and has become almost forgotten.

It may remove a misunderstanding to add that the Scotch office has not been for many years, if indeed it ever was, the only Communion-office employed by the clergy of Scotland. Bishop Torry said in 1846 that, when he began his ministerial service some sixty years before, there was but one of about sixty-four congregations in Scotland in which the national Eucharistic Form was not used; and he lamented bitterly the introduction and use of the English Office.[2] The canons of 1811 declared the Scotch Office to be of primary authority, and to be used at all Consecrations of Bishops, and forbade its being laid aside in any place where it was in use without the sanction of the College of Bishops.[3] Yet in 1819, no clergyman in the diocese of Edinburgh except the Bishop made use of it.[4] The present canons

---

[1] Life of Bp. Seabury, p. 264, n. [2] Neale's Life, pp. 315, 316.
[3] Ibid, pp. 80, 92 n. This last restriction was afterwards modified. [4] Ibid., p. 96.

of the Scotch Church, adopted in 1863 and 1876, allow both the Scotch and the English forms, giving the primary authority to the latter by ordering it to be used at all Consecrations, Ordinations, and Synods, and in all new Congregations unless a majority of the applicants desire the other.[1] At the same time, it is the opinion of those best qualified to judge of the question, that the feeling in favor of the national office is increasing in Scotland.

It is hoped that it will not be amiss to add to this historical sketch a few notes on certain parts of the office which is here reprinted.

This service departs from most of the Scotch service-books, including that of 1637, in substituting the word "Priest" for "Presbyter" throughout the service, following therein all the English books from the beginning, and the Non-juring book of 1718.

The offertory sentences are the same as in the book of 1637, one being "reserved for a form of presentation before the Lord."[2] Those which were not then adopted from the English service were "taken out of Bishop Andrewes his notes upon the Book of Common Prayer."[3] In 1 Cor. ix. 13, Bishop Seabury changed "live of the things of the temple" (the authorized version of ἐκ τοῦ ἱεροῦ) into "live of the sacrifice," which accords with all the editions of the English Prayer-Book, and has passed over into the American office.

The expression in the rubric after the presentation of the offertory, "shall then offer up, and place the bread

---

[1] Canon xxx. [2] Skinner, p. 100.
[3] L'Estrange, Alliance of Divine Offices, chap. 6, note iv. p. 189, ed. 1659.

and wine prepared for the sacrament upon the Lord's
table," was also taken from the book of 1637. The
order for the mixture of water with the wine was not in
that book, nor, as will be seen from the collation above
given, in the Scotch office of 1764; but the English service of 1549 had said " putting thereto a little pure and
clean water," and the Non-jurors' service of 1718 had
given the same direction, adding " in the view of the
people." The question of the mixture was one of the
subjects of dispute between the Usagers and the Non-
usagers ;[1] and it would seem that Bishop Seabury agreed
with the former. Bishop Andrewes and Archbishop Laud
are said to have practised the mixture.[2] The English
books gave no instructions as to placing the bread and wine
upon the table from 1552 to 1662; and at the latter date
(as will be noticed again presently) the words " and oblations " were inserted in the prayer for the Church.

One of the most strange things in the American Com-
munion-Service is that the use of the old Proper Preface
for Trinity Sunday, or even the use of the alternative
form, is left discretionary. The second form is said to
have been allowed, because the first was too strong doctrine to be altogether acceptable to Bishop Provoost; but
whether it was to please him (although he was not present at the Convention of 1789) that the use of any Proper Preface on that day was made discretionary, does
not appear.

---

[1] Frag. Liturg., i., pp. xxxvii., xxxviii., l., and references; Bulley, p. 156, note; Brett, Dissertation, p 369.

[2] Wheatly, chap. 6, sect. 11, *fin.*; Interleaved Prayer Book, p.
175. Abp. Laud's custom was retained in All Hallows, Barking,
in 1720. Brett, p. 357.

The impressive and solemn words with which the Prayer of Consecration begins are first found in the service of 1764. In the fifth line of this prayer it will be noticed that Bishop Seabury inserted "there" after "made." This word is found in all the English books, in Stephens's liturgies, and in the Scotch book · of 1637. It was dropped from the Scotch office in 1755, and does not appear again in it. It seems very probable that it was omitted from a conviction that the Oblation which Christ made of Himself was offered (or at least begun), not on the Cross, but in the upper room at the institution of the Eucharist.[1] The reading " own" for " one " is found in Stephens and in the Scotch books beginning with that of 1755;[2] the word " one " may have been changed by the Scotch bishops because it seemed to deny the truth of the continual oblation in Heaven.[3] " Memorial" does not replace "memory " in the Scotch offices till 1764. The words " and sacrifice" were inserted in both of Stephens's liturgies and in the book of 1637.

By the use of " whosoever" instead of " we and all others who," Bishop Seabury changed the last Intercession in the prayer of Consecration from the third to the first person ; and it was probably through inadvertence that, both in his office and in the American book, the latter part of the sentence retains the pronouns of the third person.

---

[1] See Johnson's Unbloody Sacrifice, vol. i., chap. ii., sect. 1, espy. p. 68, ed. 1714.

[2] By misprint or otherwise, " own" appears in several editions of the English Prayer-Book many years earlier than Stephens. Gibson, pp. 27, 28.

[3] Johnson, u. s.

At the General Convention of 1868, the Committee on the Prayer-Book reported that the confusion was not due to any typographical error, and that they were unanimously of the opinion that it was not advisable to change the present phraseology.[1]

It is very difficult if not impossible to suggest any reason for the insertion of the words " and oblations " at the beginning of the prayer for the Church in Bishop Seabury's office. In 1549, when the prayer came between the Trisagion and the Consecration, there was no mention of either alms or oblations; but in 1552, when the prayer was placed immediately after the Offertory, the words " to accept our alms [almose] and " were inserted. In 1662, when the rubric provided for placing the bread and wine upon the table (as has been noticed above), the words " and oblations " were further added, most probably referring to the elements which had thus been set apart for a holy use.[2] The book of 1637 followed in this respect the English book then in use. Unaccountably enough, the Non-jurors' book of 1718, placing the prayer for the Church after both Oblation and Invocation, says, " we humbly beseech thee most mercifully to accept these our oblations, and to receive these our prayers." This book has a prayer of offering immediately

---

[1] Journal, p. 77.

[2] So Bp. Patrick, quoted by Trevor, Catholic Doctrine of the Eucharist, p. 419. Dr. Trevor considers this to be, not the " oblatio primitiarum," but the sacramental oblation and of the same meaning as that which follows the words of Institution in the Scotch and American Offices. It seems impossible to believe that it was so intended by the English revisers. Bp. Patrick's words show that he had no such idea.

following the presentation of the alms and of the bread
and wine; so that the words " to accept these our oblations " seem meaningless, or at least superfluous.   In
1743, the first " standard " Scotch office placed the prayer
for the Church at the end of the Consecration-Prayer,
and prayed for acceptance of the alms only.   In 1755,
the passage from I. Chron. xxix. was ordered to be said
" after presenting the elements and offertory upon the
altar," [1] but the prayer for the Church was in the same
place as in 1743, and asked for acceptance of the alms
alone.   In 1764, the words of David were ordered to be
used on presenting the alms and before presenting the
elements, and the prayer for the Church was in this par-
ticular as before.   But in 1796 the words " and oblations" appear, as in Bishop Seabury's office; and there is
a note providing that they shall be omitted when there
is no Communion (a strange provision, by the way, to insert after the prayer of Consecration).   The edition of
1800 says "alms and oblations"; that of 1844, "oblations"; the two later editions, "alms and oblations."
These variations show a confusion of thought on the subject; and perhaps the change in Bishop Seabury's office
and in the present Scotch service is best explained by
supposing that "alms" and "oblations" were considered
as synonymous.   The alms are called "oblations" in
the services of 1637 and 1718 and in all the Scotch
offices.

The commemoration of the departed is adopted, with
considerable alterations, from that in the English book
of 1549.

---

[1] See the " Direction " on the reverse of the title page.

Hall's reprint does not give the full text of the Lord's Prayer; but as the change of "which" into "who" is one for which, among others, America has been blamed, it may be worth while to notice that certain of the Scotch offices—one of them, that from which Bishop Seabury took his office—have the more modern use of the relative.[1]

The Private Ejaculations and Prayers seem to have been composed by Bishop Seabury. Bishop Drummond's edition of the Scotch book, which first appeared in 1796, has similar prayers, one of which bears a close resemblance to the "Prayer to God" in Bishop Seabury's office.

As to the form of the Gloria in Excelsis, Mr. Skinner has this note:

"Of this very ancient hymn we have two editions: one is found in the Apostolical Constitutions; the other is annexed to the Psalter of the Alexandrian Bible, presented by Lucan [Cyrillus Lucaris, Patriarch of Alexandria, and afterwards of Constantinople] to Charles I. [in 1628]. As there is good reason to believe that the Constitutions have been defaced and altered by the Arian party,[2] it seems more than probable that of the two copies the Alexandrian is the more genuine. When the first reformed Liturgy was published, the Alexandrian copy had not been discovered; but after its appearance

---

[1] Bp. Wren argued for "who" instead of "which" in the Lord's Prayer and elsewhere, calling the use of the latter "a very solecism." Fragmentary Illustrations, ed. Jacobson, p. 47.

[2] They were for some such reason rejected by the Quinisext Council (Act. Concil., ed. Hardouin, iii. 1659, A, B); compare Blunt's Dict. Doct. and Hist. Theol., sub voce, p. 149.

the compilers of the present Scotch office did well to profit by it."[1]

Following are translations of three Greek texts of the Gloria in Excelsis.   The first is from the hymns at the end of the Psalter in the Alexandrian Manuscript, probably of the fifth century;[2] the second and the third are from different texts of the Apostolic Constitutions.[3]

The repetition of the clause "Thou that takest away the sins of the world, have mercy upon us," first appears in English in the book of 1552,[4] and has been retained in the English books since.   The Non-jurors also retained it in 1718; but it has been omitted from the Scotch office since 1755.   The repetition, as will be seen from the note to the translation of the first text, is not quite without authority.

Attention has already been called to the fact that in the most essential part of the service—the prayer of Consecration—Stephens's second Liturgy, the Non-jurors' book, the Scotch services since 1755, Bishop Seabury's office, and the present American book differ from all

---

[1] Skinner, p. 169.

[2] The text is that of Grabe, tom. iv., Oxon., 1709.   It may also be found at the end of Abp. Ussher's Treatise De Symbolis, Works, vii. 337.

[3] The text of the second is in Cotelerius (ed. Clerici, Antverp., 1698), Book vii., c. 47; vol. i., p. 385.   That of the third was introduced by Clericus into a note in the next edition of Cotelerius (1724) from a Vienna Ms.; but it is taken here from Daniel, Thesaur. Hymnolog., ii. 270, who speaks of the Ms. as " seriori tempore conscriptum."   See also Bunsen, Hippolytus and his Age, trans., vol. ii., pp. 50, 51, 98, sqq., London, 1854.

[4] For a reason for the repetition, see Scudamore, Notit. Eucharist., first edition, p. 710.

I.

Glory be to God in the highest, and on earth peace, good will towards men. We praise thee, we bless thee, we worship thee, we glorify thee, we give thanks to thee

for thy great glory, O Lord heavenly King, God the Father Almighty, O Lord the only-begotten Son Jesus Christ, and O Holy Ghost.

O Lord God, Lamb of God, Son of the Father, that takest away the sins of the world, have mercy upon us; thou that takest away the sins of the world,[1] receive our prayer; thou that sittest at the right hand of the Father, have mercy upon us.

For thou only art holy; thou only art the Lord, Jesus Christ, to the glory of God the Father. Amen.

6

II.

Glory be to God in the highest, and on earth peace, good will towards men. We praise thee, we sing to thee, we bless thee, we glorify thee, we worship thee through the great High-Priest, thee the very God, the one unbegotten, alone unapproachable, for thy great glory, O Lord heavenly King, God the Father Almighty.

O Lord God, Father of Christ the spotless Lamb that taketh away the sin of the world, receive our prayer, thou that sittest upon the Cherubim.

For thou only art holy; thou only, Lord Jesus, Christ of the God of all created nature who is our King; by whom to thee be glory, honor, and worship.

III.

Glory be to God in the highest, and on earth peace, good will towards men. We praise thee, we sing to thee, we bless thee, we give thanks to thee, we worship thee through the great High-Priest, thee the very God, the one unbegotten, alone unapproachable, for thy great glory, O Lord heavenly King, God the Father Almighty, O Lord the only-begotten Son Jesus Christ, and O Holy Ghost.

O Lord God, Lamb of God, Son of the Father, that takest away the sins of the world,

receive our prayer; thou that sittest at the right hand of the Father, have mercy upon us.

For thou only art holy; thou only art Christ, Jesus Christ, to the glory of God the Father.

[1]A later hand has inserted here, "have mercy upon us."

other Communion-offices in the English language in placing the words of Institution, the Oblation, and the Invocation of the Holy Ghost, in the order in which they
are to be found in all the ancient liturgies.   It would be
beyond the scope of this sketch to point out the doctrines
involved in the different orders in which these parts of
the Consecration Prayer have been—sometimes, it is to be
feared, thoughtlessly—arranged.[1]

The Roman liturgy had placed the words of Institution in an abnormal position, after the Invocation and
before the Oblation.   This arrangement was followed in
the first reformed book—that of 1549.   In the next
revision, in 1552, the Oblation was dropped altogether
(perhaps from a conviction that it was out of place, and
so taught false doctrine), and the Invocation was made
strangely indefinite by the omission of all mention of the
Holy Spirit.   The English office still retains this form.
The Non-jurors' book, taking the words of the Clem-
entine liturgy, took also the primitive order; and the
Scotch Bishops, in framing the services from which
Bishop Seabury took the office here reproduced and to
which we are indebted for our American Prayer of Consecration, though they used the words of the book of
1549, changed their order to agree with primitive custom.   This should be carefully noted, because, as we
have seen, it has been said inadvertently more than once
that Bishop Seabury followed the first book of King

---

[1] It is sufficient to refer to Dr. Trevor on the Catholic Doctrine
of the Holy Eucharist, *passim*.   On the universality of the ancient
order, see Brett, Dissertation, pp. 137, sqq.

Edward VI. in the changes which he introduced into the liturgy.[1]

The following table will be of interest as showing the variations in order which are shown by the different Communion-Offices in the English language. The several parts of the Scotch service and of that of Bishop Seabury are numbered in the order of their arrangement, and the numbers in the other columns refer to the parts of the service which bear those numbers respectively in the wide column. The first column on the left shows the primitive order of the six things which are found in all the old Liturgies and were considered essential; the second gives the arrangement when the Latin Mass was supplemented by an English Communion in 1548; the third shows how this arrangement passed over into the book of 1549; and the fourth contains the order in the proposed Scotch book of 1637, known as Archbishop Laud's. On the right of the wide column will be found the order of the present American and that of the present English Communion-Offices. The figures which denote the three essential parts of the Consecration-prayer are printed in bold type, that the variation in their order may be seen at a glance.

---

[1] Even Dr. Jarvis fell into this mistake. See A Voice from Conn., pp. 25, 26. Dr. Dix (Lectures on the Prayer-Book, p. 83) has made a similar error in saying that the book of 1637 "is still used in Scotland" and that it "gave us American Churchmen our own stately Canon."

Ancient Liturgies. [p]	Order of Communion, 1548.	English, 1549.	Proposed Scotch, 1637.	Scotch, 1755-1883. Bishop Seabury's, 1786.	American, 1789-1883.	English, 1552-1883. Proposed American, 1785.
	1[m]	1[k]	1	1. Lord's Prayer, Collect, X. Commandments.[a]	1[c]	1[h]
	19	19	2	2. Collects, Epistle, Gospel.	2	2
	2	2	3	3. Creed.	3	3[i]
	3	3	4	4. Sermon.	4	4
		4	6	5. Exhortation.	6	6[f]
	6	5	12	6. Offertory and Presentation of Elements.	12	12
7	7	6	5	7. Sursum Corda and Trisagion.	5	5
8	12	7	14	8. Words of Institution.[b]	14	14
9	10[c]	12	15	9. Oblation.	15	15
10	8	10	7	10. Invocation.	7	7
11[o]	9	8	10	11. Intercessions.	16	16
	11	9	8	12. Prayer for the Church.	8[b]	10[k]
	13[n]	11	9	13. Lord's Prayer.	9	8
	5	13	11	14. Invitation.	10[d]	
	14	14	13	15. Confession, Absolution, Comfortable Words.	11[d]	
	15	15	16	16. Prayer of Humble Access.	17	17
17	16	16	17	17. Administration.	13	13

17	17	18	18	18. Thanksgiving.
18[l]	18	19[o]	19[j]	19. Gloria in Excelsis.
20	19	20	20	20. Blessing.
	20			

[a] Or Christ's summary of the Law, in Scotch offices.
[b] Preceded by a Thanksgiving,
[c] With summary of the Law, at discretion.
[d] Followed by a Hymn.
[e] Or some other Hymn.
[f] Offertory only till 1662.
[g] Possibly.
[h] Lord's Prayer omitted in 1785.
[i] Omitted in 1785.
[j] Abridged in 1785.
[k] Lord's Prayer, Collect, and Introit.
[l] Preceded by an anthem.
[m] Hymn, Collect, Antiphons, Introit, Priest's Confession, etc.
[n] Followed by Anthem and Priest's Communion. Thus far the old Mass in Latin, the parts corresponding with the parts of the English services having the like numbers. The English part of this service began with 5.
[o] Corresponding to both 11 and 12; its position is variable. See Hammond, Liturgies Eastern and Western, Introd., chapters i. and ii.
[p] See Trevor, pp. 266, sqq.; also Brett's Dissertation.

APPENDIX.

The writer is indebted to the kindness of Charles J. Hoadly, M.A., Librarian of the State of Connecticut, for the loan, from his private collection, of another volume of a liturgical character which was published by Bishop Seabury, and for permission to print a description of the book in this place.

It is a 12mo volume, of fifteen sheets, not paged, with the following title-page: The | Psalter | or | Psalms | of | David, | Pointed as they are to be sung or said in | Churches. | —— | With the Order for Morning and Evening | Prayer Daily throughout the Year. | —— | New London: | Printed by Thomas C. Green, on the parade. | 1795. |

The contents are as follow: Morning Prayer; Evening Prayer [so much as is not in Morning Prayer]; The Creed of St. Athanasius; The Litany; Prayers; Thanksgivings; A Catechism; The Psalter: or, Psalms of David.

The services are those of the American Prayer-Book, except, of course, the Athanasian Creed, which is taken from the English Book. The rubrics are omitted, but the different prayers and other parts of the services have the proper headings prefixed. Before the versicles, the word "Minister" is replaced by "Priest," except in the Litany; and the Canticles and Psalter have the musical colon in each verse, as in the English Prayer-Book. In the Psalter, the Latin titles are omitted, and, besides a few other changes of words, there is a substitution of a future tense for the imperative mood in passages which might be called "damnatory"; thus, Psalm v. 11 reads, "Thou wilt destroy them, O God; they shall perish through their own imaginations: thou wilt cast them out in the multitude of their ungodliness; for they have rebelled against thee."

Bishop Seabury's reasons for making the changes in the Psalter are given in the preface, which is in the following words:

ADVERTISEMENT.

It is remarked by the learned and pious Dr. Horne, the late Bishop of Norwich, in the preface to his commentary on the psalms, *p.* 53. That "the offence taken at the supposed uncharitable and vindictive spirit of the imprecations, which occur in some of the psalms, ceases immediately, if we change the imperative for the future, and read, not Let them be confounded, &c. : *but*, They shall be confounded &c. of which the Hebrew is equally capable. Such passages will then have no more difficulty in them than the other frequent predictions of divine vengeance in the writings of the prophets, or denunciations of it in the gospel, intended to warn, to alarm, and to lead sinners to repentance, that they may fly from the wrath to come."

The same observation was formerly made by Dr. Hammond in his preface to his commentary on the psalms, p. 32. Supported by the authority of men so eminent for their abilities, learning, and piety, the following edition of the psalter is published with the alterations they have recommended, the imperative mood being changed for the future tense, in all the imprecations which occurred in the psalms. Besides which a few old words are changed for those which are more modern, and two or three expressions hard to be understood, are altered, still retaining the spirit and meaning of the psalm.

By these means, it is hoped, the psalms will be freed from all
objections, and used with more devotion as a part of divine service.

SAMUEL,
Bishop of Connecticut and Rhode Island.

New London,
    Jan. 16th, 1795.

Bishop White tells us that the House of Bishops, in
1789, did not approve of the "Selections of Psalms"
which were then prepared and allowed to be used instead
of the portions of the Psalter.   "But Bishop Seabury,"
he adds, "interested himself in the subject the less, as
knowing that neither himself nor any of his clergy would
make use of the alternative, but that they would adhere
to the old practice." [1]   It would seem that the objections
to the use of the "damnatory clauses" were pressed more
strongly upon Bishop Seabury's attention after the new
Prayer-Book had come into use, and that he adopted this
method of obviating them.   In fact, if tradition may
be trusted, his special design in setting forth this revision
of the Psalms was to quiet the mind of an influential
member of his congregation, who was a relative of his.

The number of passages in which the imperative is
thus replaced by the future is ninety-seven.   In a few
cases, as Ps. vii. 9, xciv. 2, no change has been made.   In
fifty-four instances, which seem to be all the occurrences
of the possessive case, the apostrophe which belongs to
that case is omitted ; and in four of these a plural form
is substituted for the singular, as in "mercies" for
"mercy's."   These methods of writing the possessive
are found in the standard English Book [ed. Stephens,
1849].   The apostrophe is used eleven times in such

---

[1] Memoirs, p. 152.

words as "thro'," "bro't," etc. There are many evident misprints, as "heart" for "hart" in xlii. 1, "help" for "held" in xciv. 18, "turned" for "tuned" in cl. 5; but certain spellings seem to have been purposely adopted, such as "doth" (for "doeth"), "dost" (for "doest"), "wholsom," "hony," "roring," "thy self" (two words), "rejoyce," "shew," "Cherubims," etc. Some of these are found in the English standard.

Following is a list of all the passages which show changes in words from the Psalter of the American Prayer-Book, other than those in the damnatory clauses mentioned above. Words and phrases marked with a * are taken from the English Book; those marked with a † are taken from Bishop Horne's Commentary.

Ps. iii. 2: "Many there are that say."

  iv. 6 and v. 5: "are" (for "be").

  x. 17: "thou wilt visit his ungodliness, till thou find none."

  xviii. 2: "who" (for "which").

  xix. 11: "keeping them" (for "keeping of them").

  xxix. 8: "The voice of the Lord maketh the oaks to tremble, and layeth open the thick forests."†

  xxx. 6: "hadst" (for "hast"; so in old English book).

  xli. 5: "speak evil of me and say."

  xli. 7: "imagine this evil, saying."

  xlii. 6: "disquieted" (for "so disquieted").*

  xlii. 10: "on" (for "in").*

  xlvi. 9: "snappeth" (for "knappeth").

  xlix. 5: "the wickedness of my enemies."†

  xlix. 10: "others" (for "other"); so lxxiii. 8.

  xlix. 14: "they lie in the grave like sheep."

  xlix. 14: "shall have domination." *

  xlix. 15: "from the place of the grave."

  lv. 9: "Defeat their councils, O Lord."†

Ps. lv. 21: "such as were at peace."
   lvi. 8: "Thou tellest my flittings."*
   lxiii. 5: "on this manner.' *
   lxvii. 5: omit "yea."*
   lxviii. 13: "lien" (for "lain").*
   lxxii. 16: "He shall be like a field of corn on the earth."
   lxxiii. 26: "wilt destroy" (for "hast destroyed").
   lxxiv. 14: "breakest" (for "brakest").
   lxxvi. 1: "Jury" (for "Jewry").*
   lxxvi. 10, 12: "restrain" (for "refrain").
   lxxvii. 6: "spirits" (for "spirit").*
   lxxxi. 1: "ye" (for "we").
   lxxxiii. 6: "Hagarens."*
   lxxxiii. 7: "Amalech."*
   xciv. 4: "all the wicked doers."
   xciv. 2c: "Wilt thou have anything to do with the throne
      of wickedness: which establisheth iniquity by a law?" †
   xcix. 1: "never so unpatient."*
   c. 1: "O be joyful" (for "O be ye joyful").*
   cii. 20: "mournings" (for "mourning").*
   civ. 11: "all beasts" (for "all the beasts").*
   cxvi. 10: "I said in my haste, there is no help in man."
   cxlviii. 2: "host" (for "hosts").*

"Judah" is thus spelt but once, and it appears seven times as "Juda." In the standard English book, it is found four times with "h," and four times without it.

As to the publication of the Athanasian Creed in this service book, it is very probable that it was not intended to be read in the service. This Creed had been omitted from the book proposed in 1785, and the majority of the members of the Convention were determined not to restore it.[1] When the revision of 1789 was in progress,

---

[1] Bishop White's Memoirs, pp. 117, 118.

the matter was discussed again; and Bishop White says in regard to it:

"The author consented to the proposal of Bishop Seabury, of making it [the Athanasian Creed] an amendment to the draft sent by the other house; to be inserted with a rubric permitting the use of it. This, however, was declared to be on the principle of accommodation to the many who were reported to desire it, especially in Connecticut; where, it was said, the omitting of it would hazard the reception of the book. It was the author's intention never to read the creed himself; and he declared his mind to that effect. Bishop Seabury, on the contrary, thought that without it there would be a difficulty in keeping out of the church the errors to which it stands opposed........The creed was inserted by way of amendment, to be used or omitted at discretion. But the amendment was negatived by the other house; and when the subject afterwards came up in conference, they would not allow of the creed in any shape; which was thought intolerant by the gentlemen from New England, who, with Bishop Seabury, gave it up with great reluctance."[1]

Bishop Seabury's intention in pleading for the permissory use of the Creed is shown in a letter written by him December 29th, 1790, to the Rev. Dr. Parker:

"With regard to the propriety of reading the Athanasian Creed, I never was fully convinced. With regard to the impropriety of banishing it out of the Prayer Book, I am clear; and I look upon it, that those gentlemen who rigidly insisted upon its being read as usual, and those who insisted on its being thrown out, both acted from the same uncandid, uncomplying temper. They seem to me to have aimed at forcing their own opinion on their brethren. And I do hope, though possibly I hope in vain, that Christian charity and love of union will some time bring that Creed into this book, were it only to stand as articles of faith stand, and to show

---

[1] Ibid., pp. 149, 150.

that we do not renounce the Catholic doctrine of the Trinity as held by the Western Church." [1]

Whether the amended Psalter and the Athanasian Creed were used in St. James's Church, New London, or elsewhere, can probably never be determined; but the fact that the first Bishop of Connecticut prepared and published this volume cannot cease to be one of the most interesting facts in the early history of the Prayer-Book of the American Church.

[1] Bishop Perry's Handbook of the General Convention, p. 76.

Breinigsville, PA USA
09 July 2010
241506BV00003B/88/P